OUR FATHER
SAINT BENEDICT

First published in the United States of America 1983
by New City Press of the Focolare Movement, Inc.
206 Skillman Avenue, Brooklyn, NY 11211
© 1982 New City London

First published in Spain 1980 as *El Pare Sant Benet*
by Publications de l'Abadia de Montserrat

Printed in the United States of America
ISBN 0-911782-45-1
Library of Congress Catalog Card No. 83-061716

OUR FATHER
SAINT BENEDICT

Text by
M. Regina Goberna, O.S.B.

Illustrations by
M. Lourdes Vinas, O.S.B.

new city press, new york

Behold Brother,
how in his loving mercy
the Lord shows us
the way of Life.

Prologue of the Rule of St Benedict

Presentation

Dear Reader, here you have a new book, in which the authors wished to let St Benedict speak in an up-to-date and simple way, in both words and pictures, since a man who lived so many centuries ago, cannot be completely understood without being somehow translated into today's language.

On the other hand, his writings, his life, his message coincide with people's longings for sincerity, simplicity, and deep values. In these times when it is difficult to find happy faces, his words inviting to happiness are more valid than ever, particularly since he has in mind not a superficial happiness, but one which is the fruit of the Spirit. St Benedict well knew what nestles in the depths of man and had had long experience in dealing with God. He knew the ways of the Lord and we could say that his work has this objective – to help man to encounter his Creator.

It is true that he was writing specially for monks, but for him a monk was, first and foremost, a Christian.

Therefore, the nuns who have prepared this book with such high hopes, on the occasion of the fifteenth centenary of St Benedict's birth, are joined by the whole community of this monastery. Together, we dedicate these pages not only to our brothers and sisters in monastic life, but in a special way to all Christians who live in the midst of the world.

For us they are not pure history or theory, they are the fruit of a long apprenticeship in the School of St Benedict and of a personal experience in community. Hence it seems to us that they may also help our brothers and sisters who live exceedingly busy lives in the daily struggle, to meet with Christ, present in their own lives, in their brothers, in the Church. With Christ, before whom St Benedict teaches that nothing should be placed.

M. CECÍLIA BOQUÉ
Abbess of Saint Benedict of Montserrat.

Contents

Foreword

"Jesus of Nazareth is passing by," they told the blind man. "Jesus son of David, have pity on me," he cried. His cry stopped Jesus in his tracks to reward the man's faith with the gift of sight.

Five hundred years later, Benedict of Nursia had a similar experience in the student world of Rome. Its university life was, if anything, more permissive than our own. Professors of every known philosophy, true and false, were peddling their wares to impressionable students. Advocates of all manner of depravity fanned their youthful passions, justifying their pupil's behaviour with fascinating theories that tantalised their brilliant young minds with half truths. But these never quite satisfied their thirst for truth itself.

Benedict felt overwhelmed by this flood of conflicting theories. Words, words, words! He longed for silence to try to sort them all out. Then, somehow, in a way that he never revealed, he discovered Jesus of Nazareth passing once again to open his eyes.

He became aware of a divine source of truth. Among the countless human words, he heard a voice offering him words from on high, a voice calling "Come, follow me."

Obedience to that call took him away from Rome to an unknown destiny described in word and picture in this book. A superficial thumbing of its pages may suggest it has been written for children. To allow that impression to persist would be to miss a profound experience of both contemplative prayer and community living. In effect this is a book for the young in heart of any age.

Drawing on the *Dialogues of St Gregory*, St Benedict's Rule for monks, and their own discoveries in his "School of the Lord's Service" the authors have relived his experience of the desert.

In these chapters which follow the pattern of Benedict's

discovery of Jesus the Word, we hear him talking to himself and to his early disciples. Under the monk Romanus, he inherited from the East that docility of spirit which enabled him to discern the golden seam of truth reaching him through the layers of worthless rock. This seam is passed from master to disciple like a precious treasure down the centuries from the Apostles. Each worthy disciple in his turn becomes a master, enriched by contemplation of the Sacred Scriptures, commented by the most outstanding of the hermit monks and bishops – men like Origen, Cyril, Clement, Basil, John Chrysostom, Jerome and Augustine – all whom Benedict classes as the Holy Fathers to whom he refers his monks for deeper wisdom than he can pretend to offer them in his Rule for beginners.

Those who have been brought up in his school will marvel at the imaginative skill of these two nuns from Montserrat. Few of Benedict's 30,000 monastic disciples alive today can have lived in such close companionship with their Founder. They seem to have pondered each of the words of Jesus in his company, almost as though they had sat at his feet, invisible guests among his first monastic disciples.

The result is a series of meditations, accompanying the Patriarch of the West step by step in his own discoveries of the Wisdom of the Word made flesh – those steps he was to hand down to us in his Rule, a mine in which many subsequent Masters of the Spiritual Life have dug as a guide to their own particular charism.

Here is a challenge to all who wish to renew their lives in the spirit of Vatican II, through those ancient Gospel values which call in question the assumptions of our materialistic lives, whether monastic or lay. Not everyone will agree with the authors' insights and interpretations, which will inevitably provoke an examination of contemporary monasticism.

If Benedict were to return today, he would surely

recognise himself in this fresh portrait, offering that seam of gold to all who long for sure guidance in the ways of prayer and human relationships in family or community life. Here is the authentic touch of Benedictine realism, presented in so lively a fashion as to be both challenging and acceptable to young and old.

Lightly to discard this gift would be to risk rejecting one's European inheritance and even a life-line, unaware that Jesus of Nazareth is passing by yet again.

Maurus Green, O.S.B.

Creative Love

Benedict is his name; it means "blessed," blessed by God. He was born in Nursia to a well-to-do family, in 480 A.D.

Eutropio and Abundance, his parents, instead of gazing only at one another, looked together to God. They lived in unity and purity, their hearts ever embracing.

Their love became a fountain of abundant life.

When they were quite old, twins were born to them: Benedict and his sister, Scholastica — a double joy for their already large family!

"Bountiful Father, you are always looking at us from heaven. We place our dear babies in your hands. As the years go by, bring to perfection this new work you have begun today," prayed their mother with tears in her eyes.

Tenderly and thoughtfully, their father, Eutropio, added: "We praise and bless you, Lord God, all-powerful Creator. As you have done since the beginning of the world, you still open to us the love of your heart."

Hope

Every spring, an abundance of plants and flowers greeted little Benedict and Scholastica, as they romped through the fields.

These two children, like the tender buds bursting through the hard crust to thrill creation with the promise of new blooms, are a cry of hope in a new life.

The hope of a tiny child in an immense God.
A young, frank hope, all dreams, open, creative, free.
An obstinate hope, unlike mature experience, determined to overcome all obstacles. A hope that if held back, grows stronger, not knowing yet the meaning of despair.

"Dearest Scholastica, do you see this strong, thick branch? One day, I hope to be like that, a valiant soldier of Christ, our true King and Lord."
"And I" said Scholastica, "I will be a white dove, like this wisp of fibre, changing Love into praise of God."

Some way off, Cirilla, their nurse, was watching, enchanted. Raising her hands, she prayed, "Heavenly Father, preserve the good sense and hope of these little ones. And make us older ones children again."

University

But their parents wanted Benedict at university and soon sent him to Rome, that great city.

From the wisdom of Socrates he learnt the value of the human person. What great dignity it is to be a man, whether a nobleman or a slave! We are all one in Christ without any kind of exception.

From Plato he discovered the supreme Good, cause of all created things. Wherever Benedict went, he met the warm gaze of the God who is caring for us at every moment. God is the one we must lovingly fear since he alone knows all our thoughts and heartbeats.

Aristotle made Benedict realise the happiness of good habits and the joys of virtue, and that a sad saint is a sorry saint.

A man, then, must keep his feet firmly on the ground but his heart in heaven, letting the joy of a life full of good works unite these two extremes.

From this early training the great Benedict grew.

Flight

No! A thousand times No!

Benedict realised that study or filling a place in society is something secondary. First we have to live. We cannot turn this scale of values up-side-down without sowing corruption. There are ways which to men seem right, but which really lead to destruction.

Learning accompanied by an endless round of orgies can only throw us off balance, a prey to our fickle, stubborn and proud sensual selves. While our minds alone are being enriched, our bodies are becoming enslaved.

We are then undone and tragically divided.

Benedict chose for ever the way of unity.

Can you imagine anything more splendid?

Man when he is unified as he was before sin, is guided by the true scale of values. First, comes the will to please God, along with the higher powers of the soul. Then, as a consequence, follows his search for all other created interests.

Benedict looked at life the other way round from most men; all other wisdom looked like madness to him. So he decided on flight. Not flight from the world, but with the world, since he took the world with him. He took to flight so as to lead the world to a better life.

Driven by an upward urge towards God, he quickly reached the summit.

There he saw a light. What was it to be?

The Searcher

Whoever searches eagerly is bound to find the start of his journey a hard one. But he must not let the difficulties make him run away in panic.

When a man sets out to meet an unknown person, the whole experience is new and strenuous. Following a call, a vocation means going forward steadily, step by step, towards a better future. Only the man who forgets himself, will find. Only the climber reaches the summit.

Neither laziness nor dodging the issue leads to the meeting, to the surprise of a life built on love. Only following the straight path, with the will not to bow to the mercy of the wind, leads to the goal.

Does it all depend just on human effort?

It is God who gives us the answer through the mouth of the prophet:

"If you are truly looking for me, my sons, even before you call out to me, I will reply to you, here I am."

Young Benedict was soon to experience this. God was already waiting for him on the summit in the person of Romanus, a good monk, still searching for God despite his years. He, too, was found by God who looked at him, full of surprise, through the eyes of that boy.

"Can you keep a secret? I want to live in solitude, to search for God in earnest," said the boy humbly.

"Yes, my son. Search for the One who has found you. Search for him in faith and one day you will see him, face to face. He has always been at your side. Here is a cave. If you wish to stay, you will just be able to fit into it standing up."

The Monk's Habit

Next day, Romanus clothed Benedict in the monk's habit. By what right? he wondered. Why give him privileges, when he desires none? Will this strange dress help him to be a brother among brothers?

Careful thought showed him three reasons for accepting.

It is the same dress as Romanus wears. So, from now on, he has a new family – a right he values.

The habit will remind him that a new man is beginning within him. As in a second baptism, he has clothed himself in the new Adam. He, little Benedict who is a nobody, has not yet become a new Adam, but he will – by vow — become a new Adam by his behaviour. The habit does not make the monk, but it helps him – his great privilege.

Then, since he is a human being, the habit will remind him of his decision to search for God. We men and women cannot live without signs. Signs are like poetry. They say the deepest things in life more vividly than words.
The brethren clearly see it this way. How important, then, is the theology of beauty – aesthetic theology!

"Lord Jesus, how grateful I am! What dignity you give me!"
And Benedict weeps and laughs for sheer joy.

Holy Tradition

Every day Romanus lowers a basket on a rope down the side of the precipice to the cave, to bring Benedict his food.

"Father Romanus," says Benedict, "this bread seems to be a warm leaven that keeps fermenting within me."

"Yes, my son," says Romanus. "It is kneaded in the love of generations of men who have loved one another and handed this bread on to each other in holy Tradition.

"You are setting yourself to reap where you have not sown, but others, before you, have tired themselves out in this work.

"Handing on love makes a chain to which each of us adds his link. The more you come to understand Love, the more you will feel bound by this narrow bond, stronger than iron or steel.

"It is the bond of Christ, our Lord."

Solitude

A chain of mountains on either side of the narrow valley, a leaping stream rushing through it, a patch of vivid, luminous, blue sky, a raven who comes daily to share his meal – this is Benedict's solitude.

Nothing else.
Alone with himself.
Alone before mankind.
Alone before his God.

Benedict has now no choice but to set out along the path of silence, of tranquillity, searching for God and his peace.

In single combat, there are no half measures.
Death or life.
Go mad or go deep.
Accept yourself or lose your head.

And in this alternative, Benedict discovers who he is.

He is one blessed by God.

The Desert

One blessed by God? No, a blessed down-and-out!
Benedict has begun to discover what he is not.

The closer we come to Truth the more false we see we
are. Benedict, faced with his own defects without any
excuses, has to bear with himself with great patience, day
after day.

Emptiness!
All the good in him comes from God. Only the bad is his
own. From the depths of his sins, recognising the evil in his
heart, Benedict is completely crushed, weighed down,
humiliated. He utterly despises himself.
Night!
Unworthy to raise his eyes to God since he is a sinner.
Insanity!
A worm thrown in the dust, a lamb led to the slaughter, a
donkey before his master.

Is Benedict now in despair of God's infinite mercy? No.

The emptiness is full of all his longings, his desires, all
his spiritual anguish.
A night spent in the certainty of being strong in him who
can do all things, of emerging the conqueror in him who
loves him.
Sanity indeed, with an understanding which can only be
the fruit of the Spirit.

On his own, a blessed down-and-out.
God-with-him! A blessed man, a man favoured by God, a
man whom grace has filled.

Silence

Not a single word.
The whole of Benedict is like one great ear listening to the voice of the Spirit who speaks to the "Churches."

Today, now, while you have the light of life, now is the moment.
Rid yourself of indolent dreams.
Awake. Be on the watch.
Gladly welcome the silence crying out to you.
It is directed to you.

"Listen, son . . .
. . . I am your loving Father."

Is it possible?

And Benedict learns that there is a Word, full of power, ever resounding in the today of God and in the now of time. The many other words do not escape sin. And he learns that because this Word is so serious he must listen to it.
If he closed his ears and let the Word pass by, his heart would grow insensitive, as unfeeling as the hardest rock, until, for lack of life, it would die.

And so, invaded by a desire for deep silence, Benedict stays very still, as often as he can, without moving a muscle. His head bent, he inclines his inner ear:

"Speak, Lord!"

Discovering the Heart

What a surprise!

Listening with his inner ear, he can make out a vital impulse within himself, constantly pulsating. Can't you hear its beats? They are even audible.

Yes. He is learning to love with his whole heart, with all his soul. With a bubbling activity. With a great outpouring of the Spirit. Free. Ever-expanding.

The indescribable sweetness of love!

Nothing in its nature is stifled.
Nothing repressed.
Nothing frustrated.
Nothing despised.

The breath of the Spirit moves through him from head to foot and foot to head. Every part of him gets its oxygen.

Everything is centred in his heart, beating with purity, docility and measured harmony. It beats with a single Love which embraces the entire universe.

His minute heart reduces everything to unity. And it puts nothing before the love of Christ.

Inwardness

And looking with his heart – for only the heart has eyes of love to see clearly – Benedict discovers yet another presence.

Every human being, the greatest sacrament of God, is like a consecrated pyx, where Christ is hidden: Christ, the redeemer of mankind. Therefore, every person is worthy of being treated with great honour, great respect, great dignity.

The tiny plants growing beside the cave, the swallows ceaselessly coming and going, the leafy trees dancing to the rhythm of the breeze, the rocky outcrops towering to the heights of heaven, the dense clusters of brambles nearby, every flower along the path leading to the valley, all breathe forth the splendour of the constant presence of the "sacred."

Like the altar vessels with the wine and wheat-ears of the Lord.

Benedict does not know what the new heaven and the new earth will be like, but he believes this mysterious transparency is giving him a foretaste.

So there alone in his cave – he dances for joy.

Temptation

What's the meaning of this, Benedict?
Dancing alone?
Have you gone crazy, letting your imagination run away
with you?

In real life, things are not what you make them out to be.
You are just the same as the companions you left behind
some time ago.
And they do not lead your kind of life.
They do not do the strange things you do.
Nor do they dally in your folly.

A brainstorm, that is what is wrong with you.
Go back to the city among normal people.
Do you not remember little Sabina?
You could set up home together, the pair of you . . .

And Benedict is weighed down with sorrow.

Imagination or reality?
Madness or good sense?
A moment of decision or time miserably lost?

Benedict falls to the ground on his knees:
"My God, my God, what is your will?"

Adoration

"My son,
You are an unfinished work,
I the Author.
You – one thrown into infinity,
I – the immensity.
You – a tiny child,
I – the Father of Goodness.
You – the insecure,
I – the rock to which you are anchored.
You – a thought,
I – reason.
You – a word,
I – the total and unique truth.
You – wholly possessed,
I – the possessor of all.
You are submerged in me.
If you could contain, understand, explain me,
I should no longer be I, he—who—goes—ahead—of— you,
Neither would you be you,
Because you would die unfinished, insufficient,
In your miserable weakness,
This is your condition."

Confronted by this graciousness of the God who, because he so wishes, fixes his eyes upon him, his ears attentive to his words, showing him with love the way of life, Benedict weeps with gratitude, in adoration.

Beloved brothers, is there anything better than to listen to that voice of the Lord calling to us at every moment?

Prayer: the Our Father

Then Benedict began to ask God, saying:

> "*Abba*, heavenly Father,
> You are totally Gift of yourself to yourself.
> Totally Gift of yourself to the world.
> Not us, not us,
> But your Holy Name
> Be blessed, sanctified and glorified."

This is his first prayer made in the heart of Jesus, mystery of the glory of God, which we have seen with our eyes.

> "Now that you have wished to count us among
>   your sons,
> Make your kingdom come among us.
> Now, in this present hour, and afterwards forever."

This is his second prayer made in the heart of the Church, sacrament of the Kingdom of heaven-upon-earth.

> "And so that all this may come about,
> Grant us your pardon generously,
> And the ability to grant it ourselves
> So that the thorns of dissension
> That often spring up among brothers,
> May disappear."

This is his last prayer, made in his own sinful heart.

Ah, Benedict! How important is this prayer! Surely Jesus himself came to this world to utter it and teach it to us? There is nothing more freely given, nothing so powerful. Repeat it then again and again, whilst you have a heart big enough. From now on, your mission will be to beg God in prayer that, above all, his will may be done.

Easter

On Easter morning, a young huntsman, was chasing a fast-moving hare and came to a halt near the cave.

"Hello, blessed Father! You here?"
"Father? Me?"
"Yes. In your face, I see the serenity of a conqueror who has stood the test. If you like, we can share the meal in my bag. There is enough for two."

They sat in silence, exchanging smiles everytime they divided the bread and the meat. At last, the boy exclaimed in admiration:
"I would like to stay with you, search for God and your peace, living and radiating your Easter light. I would like to be a sign of the Resurrection in our world, too. Not with words but with the lessons of life."

"My son, if you wish to live the Holy Pasch with the delight of spiritual joy, you will have to open yourself up to the divine light. It will pass through you without your knowing whence it comes or whither it goes, but you will experience an intense joy whenever you are willing to share it with any brother. Then every meeting will be an Easter for you."

The hare was enchanted to hear them talking like this and drew near without fear. Where people speak of life, death will find no echo.

Vocation

From now on, Father Benedict's fame began to spread and many people came to see him.

"Tell me, Father, about your vocation. What kind of calling is it?" Valentinian asked him one day. He was a very bright, gifted and determined young man.

"Our vocation, brother, is no illusion. Disillusion would soon deceive us. Not every one who comes to the monastery can be admitted straight away.

"It is not a means of overcoming your own temperament: you will have to be on your guard day after day.

"Nor is it an escape from something in life you are afraid of: there are difficulties and harsh things along this road.

"In reality, it means possessing God and being strong, searching for him in earnest and not just in imagination, till the Divine Office comes to occupy the centre of your days and nights, as a result of your zeal.

"So as to love obedience, humiliations and that submission which hides other people's defects.

"It will make you very like Christ.

"And all this has to become part of you, so that you cannot act in any other way without destroying yourself inside. Since every vocation is very personal, it means doing not what you think is best, but what is best for you in actual fact, for you with your qualities and limitations, for you as a particular thought of our God and Lord."

Kinds of Monks

Two boys, young St Maurus and St Placid, a mere boy, decided to become monks with scarcely any idea what kind of life they would have to lead. To them Father Benedict said:

"Children:
There are men who call themselves monks, but are so only in dress, because their heads, and often their bodies as well, go wandering where they should not. Looking among creatures for what they cannot find in God, they call 'holy' anything that pleases them. Always restless, they gradually fall apart in an endless chasing of their tails.

"There are others who do not call themselves monks, but act as if they were. They are loved by God and their brothers, and live in mortified and humble service. However, they are lost because of their volatile wills. Not tested by any rule, the mistress of life, sometimes alone, sometimes in groups, they are inconstant, undecided, emotional. They always want to do the first thing that comes into their heads.

"Lastly, there are those who are monks in name and in deed. They belong to that strong race of men who fight under a Rule and under an Abbot. Inspired by the same ideal, the same regulations, the same rhythm of life, they are like the beating of a single heart, made up of a multitude of personal heartbeats, each contributing to the whole the variety of his individual love.

"You yourselves may choose the instruments that seem best to you, so that your bodies and your hearts may fight under the holy obedience of God's Commandments."

The Abbot

After a while, Father Benedict came to be Abbot of these and many other followers, divided into twelve small monasteries.

Like a luxuriant tree lovingly sheltering the birds in its branches, he gathers the monks and loves them with all the benevolence, delicate affection and tender mercy of the Good Shepherd.

Father Benedict resembles its thick trunk thrusting to the sky, leading from in front by word and deed rather than controlling from behind.

"I am here to serve, not to command. Use me as you will."

His teaching is like that hidden, rich and vitalising sap spreading from the trunk to the branches, leaves, grapes and roots hidden beneath loving mother earth, a fountain of abundant life in the heart of each disciple who, with filial love and respect, calls him:

"*Abba,* Father!"

"No, indeed!"

But all are fully convinced. Unless the Body had a proper head, four feet would set out, each spontaneously pulling in its own direction and tearing the vital unity apart. Where two are in disagreement, those who depend on them take sides and rush to destruction.

This reasonable arrangement has another important principle behind it. The followers of Jesus know that he has his representatives, not so much in the eyes of the nations as among the rest of the brethren.

The Community

Together with Father Benedict, the new arrivals make up a community.

"Hortus conclusus. Fons signatus." A sealed fountain, an enclosed orchard, a garden in flower.

That brother, his head bowed like a violet, is all humility. The other, his eyes as wide as daisies, always has truth in his heart and on his lips. Next to him, yet another, pure as a lily, is in love with chastity. Further over, is one like a wild rose, all self-denial in order to follow Christ. And the one in front, warm as a poppy, never deserts charity.

The youngest, to whom the best course may yet be revealed, is like a blossom, avid for novelty. The oldest, to whom all respect is due, is a great shrub laden with prudence.

What rich variety!

Each one, unique and unrepeatable in his own individuality, the fruit of special thought and culture; every age and every intelligence demanding a different love and attention.

In no way are they a flock of sheep.

When they look at one another, they build each other up, encouraging one another to grow in understanding, each bringing his brother to fulfilment. Every source of life, of enrichment, of expansion, is contained in this sealed garden, in this tiny closed world.

Nothing important or necessary is lacking.

What a feast when they are all united together!

The Whole World

A sealed garden?
A small enclosed world?
Then, what is happening to the rest of us?

As happens when confronted by any genuine Christian life, other men are touched by example and fed by it. Then they form little cells as the basis of society. As these multiply, they will embrace the whole world.

Could we not compare mankind to a mass of small, vital nuclei giving one another a hand and uniting in a great universal *sardana**.

But all supernatural love must be practical and begin with the brothers alongside you. For your heart to be open to all, it must first take flesh in someone very familiar to you, in those nearest to you. Otherwise, universal love would be sheer hypocrisy.

The whole world would be saved, if we all loved sincerely the group of brothers around us with a deep, patient love, bearing one another's physical and moral defects; with a generous love we feel happier giving than receiving.

Such a simple idea which costs us so much, looks like a lie!

* *sardana* – popular Catalan dance.

Order

What we see in front of us is not any old group, but a Community of Faith!

Not a bunch of tourists all running to get the best place! The Community advances rhythmically at an ordered, calm pace. All in the same direction.

Like the tribes of Israel crossing the desert, lined up in formation around the Ark and following the bright cloud which moved ahead of them.
The Abbot, Christ, leads the way. Then the lines of well spaced monks. With great dignity, each one in his proper place.

– What an honour to be always counted among them!
– What responsibility to occupy a space with conviction!
– Let no one, then, be anxious or saddened in the House of God!

Order, in the monastery, is of the first importance.
All have their appointed tasks, every object its special place and each work its suitable hour. So, from this great, organised body there springs continually the happiest life imaginable.

Life, ordered within and without, is transformed into peace.

Stability

Peace tends to stillness.

Tranquillity?
Escape from complication?
Not at all!
It means a stillness free from external agitation, filled with a more intense activity of the heart.

Not novelty sought in worldly affairs, but a deepened love in the joy of the Holy Spirit, is what brings new birth to a man from on high, moment by moment.

This increased activity of the heart is assisted by living always in the same surroundings; the same house, the same faces, the same circumstances, the same opportunities. Constantly trained in the ranks of the same brothers, till everything around you becomes life of your life, sap of your vitality and an inherent part of your very body. This helps you pierce the crust of outward appearances and enter into communion with the deep love that every person has hidden in his heart.

This communion is not born of the novice's first fervour but comes through the long experience of many years.

Brother, now that you have chosen this way, there is no other solution. Your life must unfold within the confines of the monastery and your stability grow in the bosom of your Community.

Unless you follow this way, you will have difficulty in reaching your goal.

Profession

"Welcome me, Lord, as you promised when you called me.
Then I shall live for you and not be deceived."

When a man makes his profession, he repeats these words three times, so that his decision, made in front of everyone, is quite clear. And, from that day, he will have no power even over his own body.

An exchange of love?
Yes.
But an exchange involving suffering.

God is a jealous guest who does not fit into the heart of the monk alongside other created interests. When he enters a heart, he makes it burst. There is no longer any "I".

*O admirabile commercium!**
In giving himself, God becomes man.
In giving himself, man becomes God.
A mysterious transformation that will last for eternity.

Death or life?
Life or death?
Only God knows.
God and the monk who yields himself up to him.

Yes Brother! And no bandying of words or false arguments!

* "Oh, wonderful exchange!"

Divine Office

What grandeur when they are in choir!

In the centre is Father Benedict.
The monks are in a semi-circle around the altar.
"With no heart, no eyes, no voice but for that Altar where the Body of Jesus and the Rememberance, and the Hope of the Body shine for ever." (Péguy).
The praise of the entire day is simply preparation and thanksgiving for the offering of the Eucharist. It does no more than revive and reproduce the whole history of salvation present in Christ.

Like Mary, the contemplative Virgin, the monks keep on bringing the Word into their hearts to ponder it, till it takes flesh in their own lives; the Word made flesh in response to the uncreated Word.

"Brothers, let us take great care over the Divine Office.
Let nothing be put before it!
What infinite value there is in every moment of it!
God is present in every place, but his eyes look at us much more tenderly when we are imploring him.

Let us try, then, to make what our voice says agree with what we are and what we think. May it keep on transforming us completely."

The Psalms

Of all the monks, young Placid is the one who gets most out of the Psalms.

He mulls over them during that quiet hour after Matins. This attentive preparation in union with the Holy Spirit makes the Psalms part of him, like his own breathing.

Afterwards, in choir, the same spirit of Love moves him to mean every word. Then he is truly living his vocation as –

An advocate,

A man of praise,

A living sign of the alliance between God and his people,

A permanent guest in the house of the Lord,

An usher of the Kingdom, whose prayer and life are a deep longing to hasten its final coming in today's world.

In Placid's eyes, a monk is a man whose heart is poor enough to be open to all times and places, a man who lends his voice so that God and men can speak through him. This means entering into the psalms, those prayers which express the faith of Israel and the Church. Composed thousands of years ago, they have fed countless generations of men and women.

Poor, insignificant Brother Placid feels drowned in this torrent of grace, swollen by so many generations who have enhanced these prayers just by using them. Docile to the promptings of the Spirit, he lets himself be dragged, submerged and tossed about by the waves of this warm sea of prayer.

With Placid it is not a matter of reciting Psalms, one after the other, in their proper order. He loves to become part and parcel of each one. Without moving from his stall in choir, he rings all the changes of mood and scene of every Psalm.

The Advocate

To fulfil his vocation as a man of prayer, he recites the Psalms of Supplication, borrowing all the needs of human beings: those of the most persecuted and calumniated, the chronically sick and those most tormented in spirit. Laden with all these intentions, he presents himself before the Father in a daring, familiar way, humble and trusting. However crude or bold, no request, no complaint, no lament, no exposed evil deserves rejection in his eyes. Like Jesus, he does not notice how he calls the Father to account; why have you forsaken us?

He well knows that the Father greets us with silence, but as a man, he talks to him in the language of men.

If he dares to speak like that it is because with Jesus and the people, he has placed all his confidence in God. And even in the midst of the most agonising situation, he is capable of rising to an act of thanksgiving at the end of every psalm. This is the fruit of his total abandonment in the God he knows always saves in the end.

Poor little Placid! What a gigantic task he has undertaken, as a humble, begging monk! In every psalm, he is filling a sack full of intentions which he proceeds to empty out before God in a continual coming and going from the world to the Father, from the Father to the world . . . up and down, up and down.

Once he has presented them with immense love, he waits full of hope. He is well aware that none of his petitions will be attended to because he uses many words. Only the purity of his heart will gain him an audience.

A Man of Praise

The Psalms of Praise give him that feast-day feeling. He wants to dance for joy. But poetry, play, dance, drums are just not enough to proclaim the praises of the Creator who showers his blessings upon the whole world, day after day.

His eyes full of wonder at the marvels of nature, his heart expands in admiration to reach its every corner: the gigantic trees, the immense, all embracing sea, the countless swarms of animals, small and large: and, above all, man, that tiny king of creation which God has placed at his feet.

No set formula, no selfish petition. Here all is pure praise, grateful contemplation, adoration in the presence of God and his angels, for what he is, for what he has made and still holds in his hands. Praise of this God, so like a mother, who stands at the heart of it all, ordering its smallest details.

So Brother Placid feels he is a true monk, living his vocation intensely, as more and more hours pass by in the praise of God because he is great, because he is holy, because he is good, because of all he has done in wisdom and love.

With cries of enthusiasm, he seizes the baton to conduct this grandiose symphony of the universe, calling on all men and the whole of creation to join in joyous, vibrant praise.

A Sign of Alliance

The Covenant Psalms make him renew his pledge and that of God's people.

At his profession, he promised, along with the Church, the Bride of Christ, to have only one love: *"Ut nullum praeter eum amatorem admittam"* – "That I shall admit no other lover but him."

But it is always the same story: falling and getting up again, falling back and advancing, making a pact and breaking it, being holy and being a sinner. Despite man's successes and failures, the blows and the obstacles, he knows that, at the end of the day, it is God who is at work, faithful and loving, good and compassionate, for his mercy endures forever.

So young Placid comes back to reaffirm his vocation in every verse of the psalm, side by side with all who fall. He pledges his fidelity once more, setting out again along the road of goodness, honesty, meekness, wisdom and integrity, like the faithless bride returning to the husband of her youth.

He is happy in the company of all the poor in spirit, for he knows it is the poor who are the only truly rich on earth.

How beautiful to advance to the rhythm of a bridal march from the hands of God, in the name of the peoples of every century moving across the stage of history!

What a strange alliance!

The Guest of Yahweh

As a monk spending his days and nights in the House of God, he sings the songs of Sion. They tell of his joy as a guest sheltering in the shadow of the Temple, that goal of all human striving.

In the quiet of his soul, immersed in the depths of merciful love, he trembles from head to foot beneath the wings of God.
His soul has fallen completely in love with his Lord.
Outside him, he finds no rest either in heaven or on earth.

A love affair? Yes.
A perfect intimacy in his heart? Yes.
Mutual indwelling? Yes.
Ecstatic rapture in their self-giving? Yes.

And more than all this:

Beginning to make this moment eternal,
Beginning to be carried away to live only with the Lord,
Feeling it is good to be near God:
Feeling that God is his heritage forever, even if his body, his soul and his ardent heart are being torn to shreds.

And so, little Placid, overcome by so many graces, buries his head in the lap of his loving Father. And with it rests the whole of mankind thirsting like him for love.

Ushering in the Kingdom

Now he recites the Messianic Psalms. Side by side with Jesus, King and Messiah, he comes before the Father to beg that all whom he has invited may share the kingdom with him as soon as possible.

He well knows that the kingdom to which they have committed themselves, is not like those of this world. Looking into the future where this kingdom must have its complete fulfilment, he begs God to let it come soon and urgently.

May the Anointed one, the Son, made Head of mankind, grant true peace, a peace which protects the humble and saves both the poor who cry out for justice and the wretched whom nobody shelters.

May all the nations be given to him alone as his inheritance, now and forever.

Not just a spiritual change, then, but a final agreement between the programmes of the nations and the fundamental law of the kingdom.

To bring this about, St Placid has no pretensions. Humbly he stands at the foot of the Cross of Christ, whose arms stretch out in love. Crucified as King of the Jews and all the world, Jesus embraces both God and man.

Crucified with him, Placid makes himself one with the great Mediator, the great intercessor of that Kingdom which began, paradoxically, with an execution.

Work

*Ora et labora** are the two sides of the balance. St Benedict desired neither purely spiritual monks, nor simply materialistic men, for whom the monastic state would be meaningless.

Man's continuing salvation has two complementary and indispensable elements – prayer and work.

"Work and you won't be so sad," said Holy Father Benedict one day to Brother Timorous, a poor, timid, diffident, silent Goth, whom he found all crestfallen and out of sorts. For Benedict believed that work is not only of great benefit to society, but a powerful help to body and soul; an idle person's imagination soon runs away with him, idleness being the enemy of the soul!

Besides, Brother, work is creative; it makes us collaborate with God and with men in the gigantic task of transforming the world. So we need to run in the light of life while we dwell in this body and practise now what we'll be about for all eternity.

We are the ones who, with God's help, must build a better world.

And let no one try to persuade you that some works are low and degrading. You don't have to build a cathedral to do human work; human too are the most humble tasks in orchard and field. In performing them, we feel we are living by the work of our hands as our Fathers of old lived, and the Apostles themselves, those heralds of Christ.

In all work truly worthy of men, God is glorified forever.

* Prayer and work

Obedience

St Benedict teaches that every task can be done in one of two ways: either from choice or from obedience; because you enjoy it or because you believe it to be a duty in conscience. But doing a job from choice is not so hard as having to do it, since man always wants to be his own master.

What vanity!

Fancy spending the day making plans and calculations for tomorrow when all that matters is obedience! And following, not your own tastes and desires, but the narrow path that leads to life!

For there is a single will hovering over mankind and to that will we must all conform. Instead of doing so, we find, in every one of us, two wills locked in combat; selfishness which seeks what is best for oneself and generosity which leads to mutual obedience, ever affable, prompt, meek, joyful and pleasing.

For obedience is proper to those who love nothing so much as Christ.

Only Love is the great obeyer.

Young St Maurus is the one who lives it best.

Leaving his own things at once, he flies on the wings of obedience to what he is commanded:

To work? No sooner said than done. And with what results!

To clean? No sooner said than done. How everything shines!

To prayer? No sooner said than done. What holy fervour!

To take a walk? No sooner said than done. How delighted he is!

So concludes St Benedict:

"There's a monk to the marrow of his bones, his heart fixed on Christ and not on himself. Since he's the champion in obedience, I'll make him my prior."

74

Dialogue

"I your prior?", asked young Maurus, petrified.

"Yes. In complete trust, I'll share my burdens with you. If you know how to obey, you'll be able to command, listening to everthing the others have to say to you. It's good to do everything after taking advice. This will enable you to advance along the only road that leads to God: doing his holy will.

"For *Oboedire est Obaudire* – Obeying means listening.

"Yes, my son, the greatest mystery in the world is that of the holy communications, that the Word of God is expressed by the mouth of men who are such limited and defective creatures!

"In the first place, through the Abbot whose command may call for your patient reaction at the right moment, with the grace of the Holy Spirit. But his decision is final. His words are the most sure – *ipsissima verba Christi,* the very words of Christ. And you must desire to be ruled by them always.

"In the second place, through your brothers with whom you must behave with humility, gladly listening to them, searching without delay and in mutual competition what is best for all, and offering them a kind reply on all occasions. One loving word is more valuable than the most precious gift.

"Difficult, isn't it?

"Ask the Lord, then, that what is impossible to your nature, he may obtain for you by the help of his grace. If you achieve it, you will be a monk, indeed. You will be the most perfect imitation of Christ who made himself obedient unto death."

The Crisis

God took him at his word.

After a while, it was St Benedict himself who had to put it into practice and obey. He had to bow down, even before evil. No easy matter.

Where there are men, there is sin, bringing the mystery of evil into play. By this time, St Benedict's fame had spread far and wide, arousing the envy of a priest who did great harm to the servant of God and his followers.

A man's job is difficult, but failure is even more so. It is harder to be patient in the face of contradiction and stand firm in the hour of trial. It is harder to bless than to return curse for curse. Harder still to let yourself be crucified, conquering evil with love.

And St Benedict could not spare himself.

One night, he prayed with great intensity, like Jesus in Gethsemane.

"Father, you're putting us to the test, making us pass through fire like gold in the crucible, so as to purify us. You have put men in our way and over our heads. So, then, not our will but your Holy Will be done, your will which comes at us from all directions. Even through false brothers.

Into your hands we commend our spirit."

The following morning, realising that a crisis, once accepted, is a source of growth and that every death is the bearer of life, for the good of all, he would set out with a group of brothers, faithful to a new call from the Lord.

Monte Cassino: a Greater Height

He was forty-five years old when he reached the mountain which rises above the ancient *Cassinum* of the Romans.

Instead of the narrow Subiaco valley of his youth, here is an ample, open, sunlit mountain which joyfully proclaims men's gratitude for God's salvation.

Instead of the steep precipice, a very harmonious, even and well proportioned mountain. In fact, a symbol of the just norm for men – neither too high nor too low, neither too short nor too long.

Instead of the tiny grotto, an esplanade with a famous pagan temple, which will soon turn towards Christ, the unique King and Lord. A temple where the whole universe seems to rise and converge quite naturally.

Instead of wild woods full of undergrowth, the vast and fertile plain of Cassino lies at its foot, criss-crossed by paths and roads, cares and longings. A vast, fertile plain which no eye ever beheld nor heart ever guessed at, except from this majestic little city of the Spirit.

Instead of the struggle to conquer his sinful body, Benedict now experiences the peace of a naturally good man, one who is prudent, patient, and sufficiently holy to be truthfully called a saint.

Instead of a crow for companion, he now has a group of brothers who really love him in the charity of Christ.

Previously, his renown nad spread all around; now it will spread throughout Europe and the entire world.

If, at certain moments in life, we are not born from on high, we shall never reach the highest peaks of doctrine and virtue to which we have been called.

A Fresh Start

When they got up there, their first duty was to beseech God with insistent prayer, as they always did at the start of any good work:

"Father, we begin with the world which is beginning again at every instant of every moment.

With the stars which light up again each evening in the firmament, in the quiet which advances silently into the heart of each night without the slightest lurch.

With the day which conquers darkness each morning in joyful reawakening and with the sun, born again each dawn, to rise and send forth its powerful rays.

With the flowers blooming again each spring, and the swallows returning southward every autumn.

With the city coming to life again at the first light of each day and with the hearth, at eventide, gathering its sons together once more.

We start off with Love which begins each instant of every moment ceaselessly renewing itself. If we allowed it to escape, would we not cease to exist? Is life not a constant rebirth of love? Yesterday, we broke our selfishness by dashing it against the rock that is Christ. Today, with selfishness conquered, love makes us determined not to fall back into it.

If with you and with our brothers we begin today as if it were the first day, with determination and perseverance, shall we not transform our life, and the world itself, as Christ began to do? We have no wish to be soft as lead!"

Do you see them all there with their heads looking up to heaven?

They are being born this instant despite their years. They are being born from on high with a new birth.

Humility: Descent

After prayer, they work strenuously not only at building their new monastery, but also at rebuilding their Community.

St Benedict insists on this from the very beginning:

"Brothers, let humility be like the cement which binds the stones of our building. Humility has no other aim than to unite without being noticed. It wants to be there, while seeming not to be. It has no need to excel. Where there is humility, there is true brotherhood, the true spirit of community in an incomparable union.

"Humility makes us enter the rhythm of the *kenosis** of Christ who humbled himself before being exalted, who before rising wished to die, in order to reunite us all in communion with the Father and the Son.

"Humility by descending lifts us to the highest exaltation, to that charity of God which, in order to be perfect, excludes all division. This is what the Lord has deigned to teach his workman, once purified of vices and sins by the grace of the Holy Spirit.

"Meanwhile, my brothers, it is only by advancing towards the summit of the highest humility in this present life that we shall succeed in becoming a community.

"And when the heart is truly humble, the Lord will direct it heavenwards, towards that full communion with God and with his saints."

* Greek = emptying.

Humility: Ascent

For building through humility is like a stairway with twelve steps which you have to build from the bottom up.

The first step is to keep your eyes open to God at every moment, since he is always looking at us from heaven. This way, you keep your heart pure.

The second is not to love your own longings and desires but rather those of him who has called us to the monastery.

The third is to make yourself obedient until death.

The fourth, to endure everything, including contradiction, bravely and patiently without giving up, growing weary or ever giving in to despair.

The fifth, to be convinced of your own weaknesses without hiding them out of fear of confession.

The sixth, to be happy always and everywhere.

The seventh, far from collapsing because you know you are very sinful, to draw profit from that knowledge.

The eighth, to plunge head-first into the rhythm of community life with your whole heart.

The ninth, only to speak with discretion.

The tenth, not to laugh except in a moderate and mannerly way, without drawing attention to yourself.

The eleventh, when you speak, to do so in a low voice, gently, seriously and with a few well chosen words.

The twelfth is that humility, once attained both inwardly and outwardly, should shine forth always in your whole behaviour.

In this way, having climbed all the steps of this stairway which, like Jacob's ladder, rests on the earth with its other end touching heaven, we shall be naturally good men by habit rather than by virtuous effort. Fearless men who by raising themselves, lift the world up with them. Could you possibly find a better method of ensuring the ascent of all mankind?

The Tools of Body and Spirit

Every building has two faces; the outer and the inner. If we raise only one, we build on straw, so, as well as stones and cement, we must use all these other tools.

Above all, the tool of love, that total love which is a fragment of eternity, placed in a poor sinful heart, that love which is the great transcendent power of man in this world.

Afterwards, let body and spirit be stripped, by means of penance, of everything that could be an obstacle to charity. The body has to run away from gluttony, laziness, gossip . . . whereas the spirit has, to cast out murmuring, lies, jealousy, pride and anger.

In this way, body and spirit will be ready for the complete gift. The one, an athlete trained in forgetfulness of self, in clothing the naked, visiting the sick and helping those in trouble. The other, a watchful sentinel on the lookout to cheer up the brothers, loving the younger, respecting the elder, consoling the suffering and treating all as one would wish to be treated.

These are the tools of body and spirit, of the body which serves the spirit, of the spirit which gives life to the body, setting it free from every kind of pernicious slavery.

Can you not see, my brother, how body and spirit, our outer and inner man, are united? And with what holy fruitfulness for both? Nothing could be more human!

The Oratory of the Monastery

The Oratory is the place where the spirit is nourished.

In the centre of the buildings and informing the life which filters through its walls, they have built the Oratory between the guest-house and the monastery, between those from "outside" and those "within". All relationships between the monks and the outside world, pass through Christ. This is an indispensable condition. Otherwise, what would be the sense of living here?

But the completed church is in the centre not only of monastic and human life, but of the life of the entire universe, which "through the mysterious expansion of the Sacrament becomes wholly incandescent" (Teilhard).

There it is beneath the sign of the Cross, set on the highest point of the building, its arms extending from East to West.

This Cross invites us strongly to silence, to prayer, to recollection, to contemplative love.

The fact is that it is not the monks who have dedicated a temple to the Lord, but God who has built a house for them. He has united them in Community. He has given them the spirit of sonship and, as if this were not enough, each day he returns to offer them his Son, so that they may come to be body of his Body. What they have built, then, is nothing other than what they are, they and the entire world. For the human temple is the Body of the Risen Lord, with the Spirit whom Jesus has left us uniting it all in Love.

Beloved brothers, can we pray other than with tears and fervour of heart? As we gaze on these stones and these buildings, let us try to be always what we are.

The Refectory

Then, there is the refectory, where the body is nourished.

After choir, the monks go there two by two, in solemn procession.

The monastery is steeped in ritual. The whole of its life is like a Mass, and the Mass is a whole life, so that the meal resembles a second Mass. Body and spirit are one and from their union is born an offering which continues day and night.

While they eat silently in the refectory, the monks also receive food for the mind from a book that is read to them. So the meal resembles what happened previously during the Eucharist, when the Word penetrated their bodies to become Life-giving flesh, at the same time transforming them into new men from within.

The seriousness of these acts, both in choir and refectory, demands that you never arrive late. These two moments of familiar intimacy are too important to treat their value with contempt.

As a last recommendation, Brother, remember you need to be on your guard against overburdening the body.

It is quite impossible to transform a body feasted to excess. Yet you would become its slave just as surely by making it fast too long, as by giving it all it desired.

Welcome

The monastic table has one peculiarity: it is open to all. Chiefly to the poor, to those seeking God along the roads of the world, to those looking for quiet and deep silence and to those seeking contemplation of the Absolute.

No need to make a pilgrimage to India!

"Welcome, Brothers! Do come in," says Brother Valentinian. He is the Guest Master, full of discretion and the fear of God. Charitable, considerate, and watchful too against any disturbance of monastic peace and order. Here, far from the normal bustle, the rhythm of the world ceases and God's rhythm begins, that of time ends and that of eternity begins.

"Come in, Brothers, don't pass by. If you wish, we can share our prayer, our reflection and the search for that true value of things we men have often turned up-side-down. We shall live together united by those deep, eternal and sacred values. With them we neither belittle the transcendent life of faith, commitment, love, fidelity and the edification of mankind, nor do we put first those superficial things destined to die with this world.

"Pass, Brother. We shall not wash your feet, nor kiss your hands, nor prostrate ourselves before you, but, indeed, treating you with all respect, honour and veneration, we shall adore the Lord whom we welcome in you.

"As before, during the Eucharist, you are Christ our Brother come back in bodily form."

Service

St Benedict was saying very humbly to his guests: "The life we lead here, my brothers, has a double secret support like the two legs of the body – the spirit of service and the spirit of recollection. Let nothing be done to excess; neither always serving, nor always contemplating, just as a person is never always receiving, nor always giving. In the house of God everything has to be ruled by moderation and administered wisely by wise men.

"With regard to the spirit of service which we offer you so unworthily and which we also offer each other, we believe that it must have one quality, namely self-sacrifice. We must not do it in order to be rewarded by it.

"We must also throw ourselves into it with enthusiasm without hesitation or complaint, offering ourselves for any service, whether it be the most important or the most humble and hidden.

"It means being at the disposal of the least of all as well as of the most pleasing brother, serving one another joyfully, whether on good days when we are happy or on dull days when we feel out of sorts and sad.

"Finally, we have to have the same charity towards all, without getting angry with the person for whom we are a rebuke and who takes our kindness amiss, or getting puffed up because of the wish to be generous. In fact, following the Lord's advice, we must simply say, 'We are useless servants, we have done what we ought to do'.

"So, whether serving outsiders or those at home, we men come to be missionaries. For Jesus tells us that what we do to a brother we do to him, whether that brother be in Africa, at home or in the monastery."

The Cell

Then there is the question of recollection. What joy for a monk to be able to kneel down in his cell, full of fervour! In this blessed and much loved corner; in this sanctuary of the Spirit where he recovers his strength! An oasis of peace where time stands still. Every instant has infinite value, because it is a moment of great intimacy and deep contemplation.

Alone! Shut in?
No! Nothing is so universal!
Here the monk is intensely united with all those brothers going about the world doing good. With all those who, through their sacrificial and silent work, are renewing life in society, with all who, by generous and valiant efforts, are building up that great body which is mankind.

He also feels his solidarity with the weakest brothers, the most lost, most avaricious, most sinful, with the most prodigal sons wandering through the world wreaking havoc. For he too is very sinful!

As brother of all those brothers and as their servant who places his love at the disposal of the whole body, he presents himself before the Father with all that they are. All their wickedness and all their goodness. Everything passes through his insignificant heart, into which everything fits, through his heart which is all for men and all for God.

This is also a very important kind of activity, from which he always emerges completely comforted, and completely strengthened within himself. Invigorated with new life.

Is the joy of the Lord not his entire strength?

Virginity

If the cell is for the monk the hour of great love, of deep recollection and contemplation, virginity is the cell of the soul which makes sense of that love. It is his gift, with the chaste sweetness of charity and purity of heart, of his whole body. From head to foot.

It means having eyes open only to the clarity of the Light of Life, a mouth only for holy and edifying conversation, a will only to please God, to be pure in his presence, keeping clear of all iniquity. It means having hands clean of sin, and a heart full of compunction which confesses past faults with tears and opens itself to continual conversion.

Virginity is the most exquisite flower of the lover for the beloved. It means giving oneself completely, totally, without keeping any corner for oneself. It is being aware of one's actions, without being distracted by false dreams. It is loving God to the extreme and one's brothers with the same love with which he has loved us. And this involves casting out unclean mediocrity and lukewarm love.

Virginity does not exist only in the heart but manifests itself outwardly as well in the body which is united in service to the Lord himself.

Someone may say; That's for saints. Let him reach it who can! It must first be practised by the monk and then by the married. Every man of good will, whatever his condition, will strive after it.

Fidelity

How many days?
How many months?
How many years?
As you begin to live it seriously, you will feel yourself drawn, always in the same direction, always forward. The whole of your life in the same direction.

For warriors, driven by a lively desire to conquer, burning their boats after ploughing the sea is the only way out. For the man who has made a choice, fidelity to the chosen road is the only position that makes sense.

From this day on, Brother, you can no longer withdraw your neck from the yoke which you have willingly chosen after long deliberation.

Fidelity sets you free from every other burden except that of counting on him who has taken possession of you.

It is a noose that draws tighter and tighter but makes you more and more free. It dominates you. Now you can count only on him. Having set your hand to the plough, you cannot stop to look back. Blind, limited and groping, because you never see it clearly, you hurl yourself head first into the uncertain future.

For fidelity demands a spirit sufficiently strong to commit not only the present, but also the future, not only this day but the next. With a courageous challenge to time, with a stubborn optimism that is hard to shake, with a hope full of love and enthusiasm.

True love is for ever!

However, before you are truly convinced of all this, many years must go by. It is only by being faithful that you will come to understand the meaning of fidelity.

Reading

Fidelity to whom?

Fidelity to what?

St Benedict calls on us to be faithful, in season and out of season; faithful to the search for God, not to passing structures or rules which lose their original purpose. In any case, laws are only an outline, a short statement of principles. Above all, the search must continue through the Holy Scriptures, inviting us at every moment to awake from sleep. Which page of the Old and New Testaments is not a most perfect guide to human life? We shall never exhaust God.

Brother Constant abandons himself to the search with a humble heart, his spirit ever on the alert.

The Divine Scriptures reveal three levels to him, as if they were a sacred triangle whose careful balance can never lead him astray. These levels are the mind of the Jewish people, the mind of Jesus and the mind of the Church, applied to events and teachings which occurred at particular times and places in the past. These have now to be fully interpreted and wisely adapted to modern Christian life.

When he reflects with the Jewish people on the human situations in which man can find himself, Yahweh – God goes ahead of him.

When, with Jesus, he finds the key to grasp the deep meaning of past events, the Saviour acts within him and enlightens the eye of his mind.

Through the Church, all this past comes alive, vividly present and spoken to him and the men of his time. Then the breath of the Holy Spirit seizes hold of him and carries him away wherever he wishes.

The fathomless mystery of God opens him up to the inexplicable mystery of his own faithfulness in the search. Then his experiences are most unexpected and creative.

The Holy Gospels

When he feels sick at heart and realises that no encouragement can remove his malady, no correction bring him back to the way of conversion, Brother Constant returns to the Scriptures, especially the Holy Gospels, with renewed application and attention. Immediately, he feels safe again.

Is Christ not his very life?

In Mark, his faith is strengthened in the company of Jesus-Son-of-God, that Jesus who provokes more questions than answers. In this way he makes us search for him in earnest, and discover him to be greater than our minds. Then we follow him without fear until death, so as to reach the glory of the Resurrection.

In Luke, he enters into an intimate relationship with Jesus-the-Friend. Here is the Friend who offers a strong and tender friendship, humble and generous, to old men, shepherds, women, children, sinners, thieves and vagabonds. He is the Friend who sets our hearts on fire, as we journey with him to Jerusalem, the way of the Ascension.

With Matthew, he becomes the disciple of the Good Master. The Master's long discourses teach us that as his disciples, we must be meek, merciful, clean of heart, and peace-makers who love even those who persecute us. What heroism! Impossible to wish for a better programme for entry into the kingdom of our Father in Heaven.

Through John's signs, he enters the thought of Jesus-the-Theologian. These miraculous signs had penetrated the beloved disciple, as he lay against the heart of Jesus. He now offers him to us in glory so that, by the power of the Holy Spirit, we may contemplate him with our eyes.

As you watch Brother Constant with the Holy Gospels in his hand, you can easily believe that he will be constantly faithful for years to come.

The Cloister

Virginity seriously lived, fidelity to a life of contemplation practised with perseverance, the search for God along the roads of the Gospel pursued with strong conviction, demand a setting.

So, certain things are excluded – unrestrained laughter, idle conversations which fail to build up charity, lazy distractions, not only harmful to oneself but to others, wasting time with guests or visitors – outside the call of duty – and needlessly enjoying oneself wandering around outside seeking ways of escape.

In the monastery everything has to be conducted face to face with God, in order:

To live in the saturation of the delights and joys of his presence.

To desire nothing on earth but possession of him.

To find complete happiness in him.

To thirst for his love which is better than life.

To see light in his light.

To search for the water of the fountains of salvation with songs of joy.

You see, Brothers, the cloister is not a prison, a wall, a grille, but a deep well cut out of the very rock, which offers us the greatest of all gifts. A deep well, whence springs the living water that is Christ, the Lord.

Poverty

Is monastic life, then, one of privileged segregation for men who are superior to the rest of mankind?

St Benedict prefers to think it is for the poor in spirit who, recognising their original wound, know they need adequate means to live their particular calling to the full. It exists for the poor in the Spirit who live not only a cloister of relationships, of setting, of place, but also a cloister of possessions, a cloister of the heart, of detachment which begins within themselves and leaves them poorer and poorer and stripped of everything.

Meanwhile, let the vice of property be rooted out of the monastery and let no one dare to have anything of his own, neither needle, book, nor pen. Nothing, absolutely nothing, since everything is to be held in common. As befits Brothers, so poor that they share everything in common, like the first Christians, so poor that they have handed over to Christ their very bodies and wills, so poor that they can place all their trust in God. In God and in the Abbot who gives to each one according to his needs.

Not only, then, do they not have anything, but they are not able even to give presents.
Not only unable to give, but not even possessing.
Not only do they not possess, but they can not even dispose of anything either outside or inside the monastery.

Could you wish for a more radical poverty?
For a monk is simply a pair of empty open hands who has no fear of anyone snatching anything away from him.

Spiritual Fatherhood

It is justly the poor of Yahweh, those who hope only in God and entrust their paths to him, with whom he busies himself, lovingly guiding them and directing their steps out of love for his Name.

Like the eagle spreading its wings to carry its little ones, he protects them with his shadow, sheltering them beneath his feathers, taking them lovingly upon his shoulders. He himself. He alone. No strange gods assist him.

For the monks of St Benedict this lovable and loving guide has a name – the Abbot. A brother, together with whom they seek the will of God. Together with him, they gradually discover their own personal vocation.

Because, to be born anew, it is necessary to be engendered by a father. Only one. There are many masters, but only one Father.

So there is no monastic life without the spiritual fatherhood of an experienced elder who bears his own burdens and those of his brothers, who, whilst he is helping the rest, is correcting his own defects.

Since there is no greater burden than his own limitations and sins, the man who humbly declares them, receives strength to achieve his own conversion more easily. He gains strength in the very act of communing with the suffering Christ who died to save the one who was lost.

And as with all sorrow shared you feel relief, it is easy to understand how poor Brother Timorous feels sponged down and happy when he talks with his Abbot . . . !

A Living Rule

One day, St Benedict decided to write a rule.

He wanted to put in it only the customs he himself had practised, the doctrine he had lived and the teachings that had helped him, so that they might profit those brothers who might come along in the future; those who, formed with the help of many, might wish to learn how to fight.

But, since he believed in the evolution of men and times, he wished to leave a living rule. So he said to himself, "If I gather a set of laws, either they will serve to increase the dust of the archives of people who will not even want to look at them, or they will wither up those who want to follow them.

"No. At the heart of the Rule I shall insert the love of a family: brothers who obey each other with pleasure, without anyone seeking what he judges best for himself but rather, what is best for the others, and an abbot who is truly a father, loved with sincere and humble affection. A father who arranges everything with discretion and justice."

"Love," he tells himself, "is the fundamental rule applicable to everyone. Strong minds will not be disappointed nor weak minds bewildered.

That is the best field of action while we are in this world."

Laws which Divide

When they heard about Benedict's Rule, the politicians of the last days of the Roman Empire were filled with alarm.

"Our laws are inferior," they said to one another. "They will never be able to legislate for love! At most, they can ensure justice, whereas only a superior power can produce love!

"We rule society only by enforceable laws, whereas interior attitudes and true personal relations slip through our fingers.

"We never get to the heart of the matter. Instead of uniting people, we simply succeed in enslaving, dividing and complicating them.

"Yes. The Emperor must be told.

"That book of Benedict's must not be allowed to spread. It could really and truly renew society. Then our political parties would vanish."

They were quite right.

A life of love founded on the basis of the family is the only force capable of saving mankind. For that very reason, it is not only an eschatological sign to the world of the future life of the blessed, but a prophetic proclamation of the way that is already leading people to happiness here and now.

Utopia, certainly, but a utopia taught by Jesus, and one which great men like Benedict, Francis, John XXIII or Martin Luther King have always longed for. In doing so, they have made a blast of fresh air enter our world.

The Law of Love

But good Pope Silverius, when he held it in his hands, said confidentially to his secretary:

"This Rule lies at the very heart of the Gospel."
"The summit of Revelation consists essentially in this: that God is Father, that he is Love; that we are all brothers, and that as such we must love one another."

In a very filial, cordial and humble way, his questioner agreed:
"If we were to put Christian charity at the centre of all our activity, it seems to me that we would avoid all dissipation of energy in the multiple variety of our human lives. Because the only law which is truly in the heart of man and of the universe and which completely fulfills them, is the law of love."

"Precisely," concluded the Pope, overjoyed at their agreement, "Nothing is so Christian as loving. As the great Augustine says, 'Love and do what you will', which simply means submitting yourself to the supreme obligation of charity."

Love Will Never End

St Benedict's sister, St Scholastica, had been a nun, consecrated to God like him, since her early youth. Each year she used to pay him a visit. This time, in a wholly interior unity, their meeting is completely fulfilling and their mutual understanding perfect, as they speak of love.

They talk of that love which covers a multitude of sins and imperfections, because it is sincere and humble, generous and merciful. It is the greatest of all gifts. Were they to give all the gold in the world in exchange for it, it would not weigh enough.

That love is stronger than life and death. Whereas everything will pass away with the image of this earthly city, love enables us to build another city, greater because it is eternal. For when we love, we make even matter eternal.

This new kind of love is God himself who, reflected in our human nature, welcomes us in our weakness within the immensity of his pure, good and luminous gaze. His gaze for ever overflowing, in love with his work.

Then St Scholastica burst into tears.

"Dearest Brother, I really do need this consolation because I am ill. I feel that my time has come. I have met him whom my soul loves. I have laid hold of him and shall not let him go. As I was sleeping, my heart was on the watch. Now someone is calling at the door and I'm going to open it to him. Floods of water have been unable to extinguish Love."

That night St Scholastica died.

A white dove crossed and recrossed the mysterious starlit sky of that freezing February. God who had first called her, received her into his heart, where he is Love for ever and ever.

Vision of Peace

God, in his loving Providence, did not wish the twins who had been united in life, to be separated in death. It was the month of March when St Benedict gathered his brothers together and said to them:

"The pilgrimage of my years is drawing to a close, my end is approaching. Now that I'm about to depart for the heavenly fatherland, I leave you as my testament the greatest treasure in the world: the peace of Christ.

A peace full of good zeal which puts mercy before justice, thus sharing by patience in the sufferings of Christ.

A peace full of good zeal which accepts without murmuring one's own defects, whether physical or moral, and those of one's brothers.

A peace full of good zeal which leads to an effortless life of obedience and humility, whose fruit is an ever increasing charity.

A peace full of good zeal which expands the heart and makes the monk run the way of God's commandments, persevering within the monastery till death, so that he too may deserve to share in his Kingdom.

The peace and joy of Christ, the Risen Lord, who is leading us all together to eternal life.

Us and all men who long for the life of heaven. Us and the whole created universe with which we are journeying towards a new birth.

The peace of the omnipotent Creator, before whom every creature is insignificant, tiny and mean.

That peace, brothers, which gathers the whole world into a single ray. A single and indescribable ray of the light of life, the light of truth, the light of eternity.

Death

Then, St Benedict, supported by two brothers, was carried to Choir for the last time, to celebrate his most solemn Profession, his greatest act of worship. For death is the most holy liturgy of adoration a monk can offer.

It was Holy Thursday of the year 547.

Standing before the altar he prayed like this:

"Lord, Jesus.
This is the hour of the great meeting,
Of the truly Holy Communion,
Of Love right to the end.

Henceforth I shall be a true monk like you,
Fully, forever,
Always living to intercede for the world.

Today is the day
When you have given me your Body
And your Blood.
I offer you this poor body of my flesh.

Receive it according to your promise
And I shall live.
Let me not be confounded
Since it is in you I trust.

Come, Lord Jesus. Amen."

And leaving this world, the Blessed Father went to sit down at the Feast of the Great Holy Thursday in the Kingdom of God.

The Way of Our Father Benedict

This is the way along which Benedict,
The Beloved of the Lord, passed,
And which he left us as a lesson;
A way which intersects today
With the way of our world.

Whatever your actual situation,
Stop a moment, brother,
You who have read all this.
Stop to contemplate Life,
To offer a smile,
To give a hand,
To love in truth.
Stop and enter the graciousness of Love.

Do not pass by.
God has found you too,
The God within you.
Stop and enter, you too, into adoration,
Led by the harmonious rhythm of silence,
Recollection and peace.
Stop within the cell of your heart.

Yes, you too, stop and become
A contemplative in this world.
Don't be afraid.
Stop and bend your knee with love

. . . With you, I also have bent mine.